All things are possible to him who believes . . .
who hopes . . . who loves . . . and most of all
who perseveres in the practice of these three virtues

—Brother Lawrence

This little classic of a humble lay Carmelite is an inspirational guide to all Christians treading the path to spiritual enrichment and joy. The simple wisdom of Brother Lawrence of the Resurrection has withstood the test of time by permeating the minds and hearts of men and women of all ages. As Henri Nouwen remarks in the Foreword, "Brother Lawrence's life shows clearly his great openness for his fellow human beings. He reminds us in a forceful way that we cannot find God in people but that it is God in us who finds God in people."

In pondering Lawrence's life of prayer, his companionship with God amid daily tasks, his spiritual advice, the reader advances in the realization that God is the center and substance of every moment of our lives. It is that realization which produces endless joy and fulfillment. The Image edition of this devotional work is the most modern English translation available, making Brother Lawrence's message truly accessible to all.

THE PRACTICE
OF THE
PRESENCE OF GOD

THE PRACTICE
OF THE
PRESENCE OF GOD

by
Brother Lawrence of the Resurrection

Newly translated with an Introduction
by John J. Delaney

An Image Book
Doubleday
NEW YORK   LONDON   TORONTO   SYDNEY

An Image Book
Published by Doubleday, a division of
Bantam Doubleday Dell Publishing Group, Inc.,
666 Fifth Avenue, New York, New York 10103

Image and the portrayal of
a cross intersecting a circle
are trademarks of Doubleday, a division of
Bantam Doubleday Dell Publishing Group, Inc.

CONTENTS

Foreword   9
Introduction   13

CONVERSATIONS

First Conversation   35
Second Conversation   38
Third Conversation   45
Fourth Conversation   48

LETTERS

1. To Reverend Mother N——   55
2. To Reverend Mother N——   59
3. To the same   61
4. To Mrs. N——   64
5. To Reverend Father N——   66
6. To Reverend Mother N——   72
7. To Mrs. N——   74
8. To Reverend Mother N——   76
9. To the same   78
10. To Mrs. N——   81
11. To Reverend Mother N——   83
12. To Reverend Mother N——   86
13. To Reverend Mother N——   89
14. To the same   91
15. To the same   93
16. To the same   95

SPIRITUAL MAXIMS

Practices Necessary to Obtain the Spiritual Life   101

How We Must Adore God in Spirit and in Truth   104

Of the Union of the Soul with God   105

Of the Presence of God   107

Ways of Acquiring the Presence of God   109

The Benefits of the Presence of God   111

FOREWORD

In the midst of a society marked by fragmentation and alienation Brother Lawrence's life and thoughts offer a real source of healing. Every time I pick up this little book and let its words come close to me I realize that what this simple brother who lived in the seventeenth century had to say to the people who visited him and wrote to him has only gained in importance during the centuries after his death.

Our lives are fragmented. There are so many things to do, so many events to worry about, so many people to think of, so many experiences to work through, so many tasks to fulfill, so many demands to respond to, and so many needs to pay attention to. Often it seems that just keeping things together asks for enormous energy. Different powers pull us into different directions and our sense of unity and togetherness is constantly threatened. This fragmentation is probably one of the most painful experiences of modern men and women. Students and teachers, doctors and lawyers, scholars and business people, yes, even ministers and priests, all complain that life has become so busy and that it is hard to keep the pieces together. Underneath the running and rushing of modern life often lurks the nagging feeling of being disconnected, alienated and bored. Although we are busy we experience ourselves as the passive victims of great powers that control us and seem very hard to resist. Life seems like a long series of randomly scattered incidents and accidents over which we have no control. No direction, no goals, no unity, no sense of meaning. And so while we are busy we feel an inner emptiness, and while we hardly know how to keep up with the many things asking for our attention, we feel bored.

It is to this condition of fragmentation and alienation that Brother Lawrence speaks when he presents us with the practice of the presence of God. When I was exposed to his thoughts for the first time they seemed simple, even somewhat naïve and unrealistic, but the deeper I entered into them and the longer I reflected on them, the more I became aware that Brother Lawrence's advice to walk constantly in the presence of God is not just a nice idea for a seventeenth-century monk but a most important challenge to our present-day life situation.

For Brother Lawrence, to live in the presence of God was his only concern. In the presence of God life became very simple for him. This simpleness of life, however, was the result of a long struggle. Brother Lawrence leaves little doubt that the simple is very difficult, that to be free for God asks for discipline, and that the practice of the presence of God asks for the determination to let go from many daily worries. He writes: "Having found different methods of going to God and different practices to attain the spiritual life in several books, I decided that they would serve more to hinder than to facilitate me in what I was seeking—which was nothing other than a means to be wholly God's. This made me decide to give all to gain all; so after having given all to God in satisfaction for my sins, I began to live as if there were no one in the world but Him and me." (See page 87.)

The great mystery of prayer, as the life of Brother Lawrence shows, is that this single-minded concern for God does not lead us away from people but, to the contrary, closer to them. Brother Lawrence's life shows clearly his great openness for his fellow human beings. He reminds us in a forceful way that we cannot find God in people but that it is God in us who finds God in people. When we are concerned with God and God alone then we discover that the God of our prayer is the God of our neighbor. Therefore: The closer we come to God, the closer we come to each other. When we look at the world as a great wagon wheel of which we are the spokes and God the hub, it becomes clear that our first task is to remain anchored in the hub. There in the center we find ourselves most closely connected with each other. From that center in which we are all rooted the force comes forth that makes the wheel turn. Brother Lawrence lived this knowledge and gave it very concrete form in his daily life.

One of the most stimulating aspects of this precious book is Brother Lawrence's deep conviction that prayer is not saying prayers but a way of living in which all we do becomes prayer. We indeed are called not just to say prayers but to live a prayerful life. A prayerful life is a life in which all we do—eating and drinking, working and resting, playing and praying—is done to the glory of God and God alone. Prayers can often help us very much to lead a prayerful life, but that is only a part of it. For Brother Lawrence the practice of the presence of God was not a practice for a few moments a day, not even for a few hours a day. No, for him it was a practice that permeated every moment of his day. He felt that his work in the kitchen and his occasional trips were in no way less prayer than his hours in the church. Through the practice of the presence of God nothing, absolutely nothing, was outside his intimate relationship with God. That is how he could experience an ongoing sense of joy and a real sense of communion. Brother Lawrence indeed lived a life of connectedness, which is the opposite of alienation, and a life of unity, which is the opposite of fragmentation.

This simple but difficult way of Brother Lawrence is indeed a great challenge for us today. It is a hard way but a way worth following. It is the way to God.

HENRI J. M. NOUWEN

INTRODUCTION

During the past few years there has been a tremendous revival of interest in things spiritual. Following the era of disillusionment and cynicism of the sixties, there came the realization that too often the proponents of change at any cost had gone too far in many areas, particularly in their belief that the past was dead and had nothing to offer for contemporary men and women.

The extraordinary upsurge of religious feeling that has characterized the present decade has as one manifestation a renewed interest in the great spiritual classics. Works of solid and enduring spiritual worth that had been discarded with the pietistic trivialities of the forties and fifties enjoyed a renaissance in the late sixties and into the seventies and made the great spiritual classics of the ages best sellers once again. As they had done so often in the past, their undoubted merit and intrinsic worth insured continued interest in them.

This new appreciation of the worth and role in present-day life of the great spiritual classics extended not only to the giants of spiritual literature but also to other spiritual writers whose works had a message for twentieth-century seekers of spirituality. And this little volume of Brother Lawrence of the Resurrection deserves an honored place in any such listing.

Published originally at the end of the seventeenth century, *The Practice of the Presence of God* has endured for almost three centuries and today is more widely read than ever. Though by no means to be ranked with the giants of spirituality, such as Augustine's *Confessions* or the great mystical classics of Teresa of Avila and John of the Cross, it has nevertheless firmly ensconced itself in that enduring body of spiritual works with which Christianity has been blessed over the centuries. It has now acquired the status of a minor spiritual classic that has been of great help to many in their quest for spiritual perfection.

It has achieved this honored status in spite of the curious chain of circumstances in which it became enmeshed at its publication and which effectively cut it off from a large portion of the Christian world. We will discuss this later in this Introduction. Suffice it to say here that *The Practice of the Presence of God* deserves the present high regard in which it is held and is worthy of consideration by anyone interested in advancing his or her spiritual life.

Particularly to be stressed is that these words of spiritual wisdom did not emanate from a theoretician in an ivory tower. Everything in *The Practice* is based on the actual experiences of Brother Lawrence, from the dark despair he endured in his first decade of his life in religion with the Carmelites ("I must tell you, though, that during the first ten years I endured great suffering") to the ineffable happiness and joy he experienced during the last forty years of his life ("I suddenly found myself changed and my soul, which up till then was always disturbed, experienced a profound interior peace . . ."). How he was able to turn his despair to peace and happiness through the practice of the presence of God, and how that presence can be achieved is the basic theme of all his writing—conversations, letters and maxims. Union with God, of course, is what all believers constantly seek, so this blueprint of how one man succeeded in achieving this union can be extremely worthwhile to anyone earnestly seeking that incomparable goal.

Behind every literary endeavor is a man or a woman, and knowing something about an author often helps us understand his works. Who was this Brother Lawrence, and what do we know of him?

The Man

Not too much is known about Brother Lawrence, and most of what we do know of him comes from his own writings and the Eulogy delivered by Abbé Joseph de Beaufort on the occasion of Brother Lawrence's death. Unfortunately, much of the information is either obscure or contradictory.

For example, traditionally, Brother Lawrence's birth has been given as 1611. But in a letter he wrote (according to its chronological position in the original collection) in 1686 he said, "I am approaching 80 [years]" which would have made the year of his birth 1606. Yet in his first Conversation, which took place in 1666, he said he had been converted forty years earlier when he was eighteen, which would have made his birth year 1608. But according to the necrology of his monastery in Paris, he was born in 1614. Quite probably this latter date is correct.

At any rate, he was born in Hérimesnil, Lorraine, France, and christened Nicholas. His family name was Herman and his parents, both very religious, raised him in a religious atmosphere. At the age of eighteen, he became a soldier in the forces of Lorraine and served with them in the Thirty Years War. He was captured by enemy troops, charged with being a spy and threatened with hanging. He was able to convince his captors that he was innocent of the charges and was released. He rejoined his command and soon after was wounded in a skirmish with Swedish soldiers in Rambersville in Lorraine.

This ended his military service and he left the army and returned home. However, it did not end his memories of the war. As is true of all wars, and religious wars in particular, the fighting in the Thirty Years War was savage, and monstrous atrocities were committed on all sides. Though he probably did not actually participate personally, he must have at least witnessed some of the terrible acts that men commit in the passions of war. But the memory of them so haunted him that he decided to devote his life to Christ.

For a while he served as footman to William de Fieubet, treasurer of the king of France, in which position he described himself as "a clumsy lummox who broke everything" and decided this was not for him. Encouraged by an uncle who was a Carmelite, he decided to become a Carmelite friar. But before he could act on this decision, he met a wealthy man who had renounced his wealth to follow the eremitical way of life, and he decided this was the life for him.

However, this period as a hermit only served to confuse him further, and he decided he belonged in some religious congregation where his spiritual life would have some kind of order to it. He went to Paris and applied for admission as a lay brother at the monastery of the Discalced Carmelites on rue de Vaugirard. He was accepted, given the name Brother Lawrence of the Resurrection and two years later, in 1642, was professed.

He was assigned menial tasks by his superiors, serving in the kitchen for many years, and when a painful, chronic gout developed into an ulcerated leg that forced him to walk with a pronounced limp, he was transferred to the shoe-repair shop. He accepted all assignments, however lowly, uncomplainingly and with high good spirits.

As the years passed he acquired a reputation for holiness that spread far beyond the monastery's walls. He early had a great devotion to Mary and the Blessed Sacrament, but as he recounts in his fifth Letter, his first decade in religious life was years of spiritual anguish. Slowly, painfully he advanced in the spiritual life until suddenly one day he experienced a most profound peace—a peace that was to be his the rest of his life as he experienced and practiced the presence of God in this world.

Of humble mien, he lived in the greatest simplicity. He never sought the public spotlight and tried always to lead a quiet, secluded life. But he was always available to help his fellow men and women in any way he could. Evidently of a rough exterior—as we have already noted, he called himself a "clumsy lummox," and Fénelon, the noted French theologian, after he met Lawrence, called him "gross by nature"—his holiness and concern shone through that blunt gruffness and roughness so that Fénelon concluded his remarks about him by saying "and delicate by grace. The mixture is agreeable and shows God in him." After a painful illness he died in the monastery on February 12, 1691. His life was a perfect example of a holiness that could not be contained, blazing forth from a simple creature living in obscurity and performing the most humble tasks. He profoundly influenced the lives of all who came into contact with him and, through his writings, generations of men and women after his death.

THE BOOK

Strictly speaking, in the modern sense, *The Practice of the Presence of God* is not really a book at all. Actually it is a collection of varied material gathered together by Abbé Joseph de Beaufort, vicar general of Cardinal Louis Antoine de Noailles (who was to become archbishop of Paris in 1695) and superior of the monastery in which Brother Lawrence spent his life in religion. He was early touched by the holiness of the humble lay brother and on the latter's death undertook to publish his writings.

Unfortunately, Brother Lawrence wrote little and destroyed most of what he wrote because he felt it unworthy. Consequently, when Abbé de Beaufort, at the urging of those who had read some of Brother Lawrence's letters and other writings, attempted to put together some of the friar's writings he was able to obtain only some of these letters (sixteen in all), some fragments of meditations and some recollections of conversations he himself had had with Brother Lawrence (four). It is this material—Conversations, Letters and Spiritual Maxims—that comprises the book we know as *The Practice of the Presence of God*.

Of the sixteen letters, most of them (thirteen) were written to a nun; two were to a woman in the world; and one was to a priest. But all of them are perfectly suitable for anyone interested in the spiritual life since their teaching and application are universal. And finally, the maxims are a collection of Brother Lawrence's from his writings, much of it from the letters and conversations. The reader will see at once material in the maxims from the letters and conversations.

As originally published the Spiritual Maxims and Letters appeared first and in that order; the Conversations were published in a second volume as explained below. However, I have felt it advisable to rearrange the order of the writings into Conversations, Letters and Spiritual Maxims as reading them in this sequence seems the best way to learn Brother Lawrence's practice of the presence of God and his spiritual advice. It seems particularly apt to conclude the volume with the Spiritual Maxims since they really constitute a summing up of Brother Lawrence's teaching, and as we have already indicated, much of the material is drawn from the Conversations and the Letters.

We mentioned earlier that almost immediately on publication *The Practice* was suspect by a goodly portion of Christianity. This unhappy state of affairs came about through no fault of Brother Lawrence's but did result in a disinterest by most of Brother Lawrence's coreligionists—Catholics. That such an attitude should develop toward the writings of a man who unquestioningly and unhesitatingly accepted the edicts of his superiors and his Church and was a member of one of the most stalwart religious orders in that Church is one of those ironies of history. Here is how it came about.

Abbé de Beaufort's first collection of Brother

Lawrence's writings appeared in 1692, the year after Brother Lawrence's death, and was titled *Maximes spirituelles . . . avec l'abregé de la vie de l'auteur, et quelques lettres qu'il a écrites. . . .* It contained the Letters and Maxims contained in this present volume together with the Eulogy by the Abbé we have already mentioned. In 1694 he published *Les Moeurs et entretiens du Frère Laurent de la Resurrection . . .* which contained the Conversations in this present volume together with *Les Moeurs* which was really an expansion of Abbé de Beaufort's Eulogy in the first volume. This volume was published with the approbation of the then Bishop Louis Antoine de Noailles of Châlons. The spoken and written material in these two volumes by Brother Lawrence himself consisted of the Conversations, the Letters and the Spiritual Maxims, and it is this material we know as *The Practice of the Presence of God.*

Both collections by Abbé de Beaufort were published at the time the Quietist controversy was raging in Europe and particularly in France. According to the tenets of Quietism, perfection is to be achieved by complete passivity of the soul before God and the absorption of the individual in the divine love. So complete is this absorption that the will is totally annihilated and all effort or desire for effort ceases. Consequently, the individual cares for neither heaven nor hell nor his salvation, has no desire for virtue, love of Christ or adoration of the Divine Persons, and makes such outward signs as acts of mortification, almsgiving and confession unnecessary. One further most important corollary of this teaching is that once an individual has achieved the state of passivity, sin is impossible. He or she may be compelled by the devil to commit actions that are sinful in others, but since the will has been completely annihilated they are not sins for him or her.

Quietism was the mystical teaching of Miguel de Molinos, a Spanish priest, as expounded in his *Spiritual Guide*, published in 1675, which became the handbook of Quietism. He was tried in Rome in 1685 and sentenced to life imprisonment for heresy. Some sixty-eight of his propositions were condemned.

In France, Madame Jeanne Marie Bouvier de la Mothe Guyon became Molinos' ardent disciple and taught a mitigated form of Quietism. A contemporary, François Hébert, a curé at Notre Dame in Versailles and Bossuet's confessor during the last years of his life, who had earlier been sympathetic to Madame Guyon, described her brand of Quietism: "All spirituality is reduced to the simple working of God in oneself, and in a complete indifference to everything, even to virtue and to one's own salvation, and in a complete abandonment to the will of God as regards reprobation and eternal happiness. According to these principles, it is no longer necessary to meditate on the great truths of the Gospel or on the mysteries of the life and death of Jesus Christ." Madame Guyon herself in her *Les torrents spirituels* put it this way: "Complete abandonment which is the key to the interior life, excludes nothing, neither death, nor life, nor perfection, nor salvation, nor Paradise, nor Hell . . ."

In 1687 she was arrested with a companion, Friar François Lacombe, and accused of immorality and heresy. Lacombe spent twelve years in prison and only the intercession of Madame de Maintenon with Louis XIV saved her. When her teaching was denounced in 1695, in the Articles d'Issy of which Jacques-Benigne Bossuet, the great churchman and theologian, was the chief architect, Madame Guyon was ordered to be confined (she was not released until 1703) and to have no further communications regarding her teachings. François de Salignac de la Mothe Fénelon, the noted theologian and archbishop of Cambrai, came to her defense in his *Explication des maximes des saints sur la vie interieure*, and the battle of the titans, Bossuet and Fénelon, was joined.

The struggle between the opponents and proponents of Quietism, many of them in high positions, resulted in a bitter conflict that rocked France. It raged on for years until finally, in 1699, Pope Innocent XII issued a Brief condemning certain errors in Fénelon's *Explication* as likely to mislead the faithful, particularly Fénelon's statement that in a habitual state of pure love there is no place for the hope of salvation. However, the Brief did not condemn Fénelon for heresy, and rather than settle the matter once and for all, the disagreements simmered on for years.

In the midst of these conflicts Abbé de Beaufort's two collections of Brother Lawrence's works appeared, and since one of Lawrence's basic theses is complete abandonment to the will of God, he and his works became linked to Quietism. Though some

23

aspects of Brother Lawrence's teaching bear a surface resemblance to Quietism, a more thorough examination of *The Practice* reveals a basic difference to the tenets of Quietism, which had led to the latter's condemnation. In 1697 de Beaufort published a short book defending Brother Lawrence and his teaching, giving the impression the book must be tainted by Quietism if a defense was necessary. Also, as we have earlier pointed out, de Beaufort's superior, Cardinal de Noailles, had given his approbation to one of de Beaufort's collections of Brother Lawrence's works; but in 1695 the Cardinal had come under suspicion of being sympathetic to Jansenism. This, of course, had nothing to do directly with Brother Lawrence, but his editor was connected with the suspected Cardinal as vicar general. Even in the seventeenth century, guilt by association—even for a dead author—could have fateful consequences. And finally, in 1699 a volume containing Brother Lawrence's writings and writings by Madame Guyon appeared. This, coupled with the fact that Madame Guyon had attempted to justify her theories with Lawrence's writings, was just one more evidence to many of a definite link between Lawrence's writings and Quietism.

The upshot of all this was that *The Practice of the Presence of God* never became fully accepted by the Catholic community. It was a case of guilt by association, though the association was tenuous indeed.

On the other hand, *The Practice* was taken up by other Christian denominations. It spread to England where it enjoyed a modest success in numerous editions, and over the years it was also published in various Catholic areas in Europe. It has always been available in some edition since it was first published almost three centuries ago and is presently enjoying a quiet revival in the United States. Meanwhile, the Quietism controversy has faded into history, and gradually Brother Lawrence's little volume is being read throughout the entire Christian world for its own merit despite the imagined association of three centuries ago. This edition is an attempt to spread its message one step farther.

THE PRACTICE OF THE PRESENCE OF GOD

As we have previously indicated, *The Practice of the Presence of God* is not a book in the sense that the author sat down and produced an ordered presentation of his thoughts on the spiritual life. Since it is a collection of only those writings that were available after Brother Lawrence's death, it has all the flaws of such a collection—rambling in places, repetitious, sometimes contradictory in factual matters, and often failing to develop a thought just as the reader's attention is most engrossed and wants further insights.

But despite such shortcomings there is a strength and surprising unity and always spiritual guidance that justifies its inclusion among the classic works of spirituality. Further, it has in common with all literary works of lasting value a timelessness that makes it as relevant and rewarding today as it was three hundred years ago; and I daresay it will be just as relevant and rewarding three centuries from now.

It seems to me the reason for this is essentially threefold. First and foremost is the author's simplicity of style. Brother Lawrence was neither an intellectual nor a *littérateur*. What he had to say he said simply and forthrightly and with little finesse—often with a telling bluntness. In a letter to a nun he says, "You are not the only one to be troubled with wandering thoughts." Again, to a woman in the world he wrote, "We have little time to live; you are almost 65 and I am approaching 80." In another letter he bluntly advises a nun, "Be satisfied with the state God has designated for you." And one more quotation, "Practice its [a book he had sent her] teachings in your old age. It is better late than never." The entire work is characterized by a straightforwardness and simplicity devoid of the literary flourishes that often date a work and in later times cause it to fall into the limbo of forgotten books. Lawrence's style is understandable to anyone, anywhere, anytime.

Second, and as a consequence of this simplicity is the fact that the author comes through in the writings so that the reader gets to know the man behind the letters, the conversations, the maxims. Here is a plain, humble, unassuming man beset by the difficulties we all have to endure, struggling to find his way through life, stumbling and falling but managing always to right himself, and above all keeping firmly before him, through all his vicissitudes, the final goal of life—knowing and loving God so that he may be worthy of celestial union with Him in eternity.

And therein lies the third of my reasons for Brother Lawrence's universal appeal. Here is a man who has found a way to be always in the presence of God. We feel it and we know this is so as we read his words. Without pretension or flourish he shows us his way, and we see it unfold as we read how he has succeeded in acquiring and practicing continually this presence of God. Nothing inspires and teaches like example, and these pages are alive with one man's experience in achieving the spiritual life that we all long for. Here is not a theoretical treatise but a practical guide by one who has lived every word of it.

The teaching of this humble friar is to be found in the following pages so I do not propose to discourse on it at any length. Indeed, since the compass of this work is so relatively short, it would be presumptuous on my part to tell the reader what he or she is about to read. But I do think a few short observations are in order.

For Lawrence the ultimate goal of every soul is union with God. Though he knew the perfect union can take place only after death, he believed we can achieve a far greater degree of unity with God in this life than most people think is possible. The way to accomplish this is through practicing the presence of God.

To achieve the presence of God is no easy task and the path is strewn with numerous pitfalls and constant difficulty. Consequently, we must labor constantly and exert every effort at all times to effect this happy state. To do so, two things are essential.

The first of these is to abandon oneself completely to God. Over and over again in his letters and conversations he stresses the importance of complete trust and confidence in God's goodness and mercy. "We must trust God once and for all and abandon ourselves to Him alone," "It is necessary to put our complete trust in God," "we should surrender ourselves in things temporal and in things spiritual, entirely and with complete abandonment to God," "we have a God of infinite goodness who knows what we need" are just a sampling of the exhortations running throughout the entire work.

Along with this total abandonment must go a complete acceptance of God's will with equanimity and resignation. No matter what troubles and ills come our way, they are to be willingly and indeed joyously endured since they come from God, and God knows what He is doing.

This trust must be unreserved with no thought of reward, but inevitably God will reward the person who so believes and endures with graces and treasures far beyond any sacrifices or offerings he or she has made since He is infinitely good. Also, God never tests us beyond our ability to endure and, as a matter of fact, bestows on us graces that will enable us to endure as we show our acceptance of whatever He sends our way.

Simultaneously with this abandonment to God is the constant conversation we should carry on with Him on all matters however great or small and in all conditions. By continual conversation we are able to invoke God's presence with us at all times. It is not easy to develop this habit of continual conversation with God, but we must persevere and suddenly one day we will succeed.

This conversation must be carried on not only at times formally set aside for prayer but in the midst of all our activities however menial they might be. Indeed, as his spiritual life advanced Lawrence found formal times for prayer appealed to him less than his constant appeals to God regardless of what task he was performing.

Above all, the way to God is by faith. "All things are possible to him who believes" declares Lawrence, and a bit later on after discussing ways of adoring God, he concludes, "All these acts of adoration should be made by faith." It is this faith that enables us to live up to Lawrence's admonition that "in justice we owe Him all our thoughts, our words, and our actions."

Repeatedly he stresses the difficulties for those who attempt to follow his practice of the presence of God. But the rewards are beyond our wildest imagination for by it the soul comes to a knowledge of God that surpasses all other human experiences. Always down to earth and realistic, though, Brother Lawrence is aware that "few persons attain this state; it is a grace which God grants only to certain chosen souls since this simple gaze [the interior gaze by which the soul comes to know God] is a gift freely bestowed by Him." For these few the experience is sublime. But even those who do not attain this favored state will benefit from striving for it. In closing his maxims, Brother Lawrence puts it this way: "He usually gives it to souls which are disposed in that direction and if He does not give it, one can at least, with the help of His ordinary graces, acquire by the practice of the presence of God a way and a state of prayer which very closely approaches this simple gaze."

In short, the practice of the presence of God can benefit all souls wherever they may be on the path to perfection and in their quest for union with God. It is a practice that can benefit anyone who undertakes it.

JOHN J. DELANEY

THE PRACTICE
OF THE
PRESENCE OF GOD

CONVERSATIONS
WITH BROTHER LAWRENCE

FIRST CONVERSATION

August 3, 1666

Today I saw Brother Lawrence for the first time. He
told me: That God had granted him an exceptional
grace in his conversion which took place, while he
was still in the world, when he was eighteen. He
told me that one day while looking at a tree stripped
of its leaves, and reflecting that before long its leaves
would appear anew, then its flowers and fruits
would bloom, he received an insight into the providence and the power of God which was never erased

from his soul; that this insight had completely detached him from the world, and gave him a love for God so great that it had not increased at all in the forty-odd years that had passed since he had received this grace.

That he had been a footman to M. de Fieubet, the royal treasurer, and was a clumsy lummox who broke everything.

That he had desired to become a religious, thinking that by doing so he would be censured for his clumsiness and faults and so would sacrifice his life and all its pleasures to God; but that God had outwitted him and in his religious life he had found nothing but satisfaction; that this had often made him say to God: "You have outwitted me."

That we should establish ourselves in the presence of God by continually talking to Him, that it was a shameful thing to allow thoughts of trivial things to break into this conversation.

That we should feed our souls on lofty thoughts of God, and so find great joy in being with Him.

That we should enliven our faith; that it was a pitiable thing that we had so little faith; and that instead of taking it as their rule of conduct men amused themselves with petty devotions which changed from one day to another; that the way of faith was the spirit of the Church and it could lead to a high state of perfection.

That we should surrender ourselves in things temporal and in things spiritual, entirely and with complete abandonment to God and take our happiness in doing as He wills whether He leads us by suffering or by consolation, for they are all the same to the soul truly resigned to His will. That we must hold fast to our faith in those periods of spiritual aridity by which God tries our love for Him. It is then that we should make proper acts of resignation and abandonment, a single one of which advances us spiritually.

That he was not shocked at the misery and sin he heard about every day but on the contrary, considering the malice of which the sinner is capable, he was surprised there was not more of it. He prayed for the sinner but knowing God could right the matter whenever he wished, he did not allow himself to be too upset.

That in order to become abandoned to God in the manner He wishes us to, we must watch carefully our impulses which affect our spiritual life as well as our mundane activities; that God would give light in this matter to those who truly desire to be united to Him; that if I had this desire, I could come to him [Brother Lawrence] whenever I wished without fear of bothering him; but if not I should not come to him.

SECOND CONVERSATION

September 28, 1666

That he was always governed by love, with no other interest, and without concerning himself as to whether he would be damned or saved. But having resolved to make the love of God the end of all his actions, he found this decision most satisfactory. That he was gratified when he could pick up a straw from the ground for the love of God, seeking Him alone and nothing else, not even His gifts.

That this behavior of his soul caused God to

grant him endless graces but that in taking the fruit of these graces, that is to say the love that arose from them, he had to reject their appeal knowing that was not God, since he knew by his faith that God was infinitely greater than this and than whatever else he felt. By doing this a marvelous struggle between God and the soul took place; God giving and the soul denying that what it was receiving was God. That in this battle, the soul, because of its faith, was as strong or stronger than God since He could never give so much that it could not deny that what He gave was Himself.

That his ecstacy and rapture were only those of a soul which played with these gifts, instead of rejecting them and going on to God. That beyond the wonderment, one must not let oneself be carried away; that God was still the master.

That God repaid everything he did for Him so promptly and so munificently that he sometimes desired to be able to hide what he did for His love since by not receiving a reward, he would have the pleasure of doing something solely for God.

That his spirit had been deeply troubled since he was certain he would be damned; that all the men in the world would have been unable to convince him otherwise; but that he had reasoned about his feeling in this way: "I have entered the religious life solely for the love of God. I have tried to live only for Him; whether I am damned or saved, I desire always to continue to live only for the love of God; I shall at least be able to say, right up to my death, that I have done my utmost to love Him." That this

39

melancholy thought had been with him for four years and had caused him intense suffering.

That since then he had not concerned himself about either heaven or hell and his life was free of worry and full of love. That he had put his sins between God and himself, as if to tell Him he did not deserve His favors, but that God continued to shower him with His blessings. That He sometimes took him by the hand and led him before the entire court of heaven to reveal to all the wretch on whom He so graciously bestowed His graces.

That in the beginning a persistent effort is needed to form the habit of continually talking with God and to refer all we do to Him but that after a little care His love brings us to it without any difficulty.

That he expected, after the happiness God had given him, that he would experience pain and suffering, but that he had not worried about it knowing well that since he could do nothing by himself, God would not fail to give him the strength to bear the pain and the suffering.

That when the occasion arose to practice some virtue he always said to God: "My God, I cannot do this unless You enable me to do so" and he was immediately given the strength needed, and even more.

That when he had stumbled, he simply acknowledged his fault and said to God: "I shall never do otherwise if You leave me to myself; it is up to you to keep me from falling and to correct what is wrong." With this he put the pain of this fault from his mind.

That we must act very simply with God, and

speak to Him frankly, while asking His help in things as they occur; that God never failed to give it, as he often found out.

That he had recently been sent to Burgundy to buy wine, that this was difficult for him since he had no head for business matters, he was lame in one leg and could not get about on the boat except by hobbling from one cask to another but that he had let none of this bother him, least of all the purchase of the wine. That he said to God that it was His business he was on, and that afterwards he found out everything had gone smoothly and he had done well. That the previous year he had been sent to Auvergne for the same purpose; that he did not know how the business was accomplished, but accomplished it was and very well indeed.

The same thing was true of his work in the kitchen, for which he had a naturally strong aversion; having accustomed himself to doing everything there for the love of God, and asking His grace to do his work, he found he had become quite proficient in his culinary chores during the fifteen years he had worked in the kitchen.

That he was now in the shoe repair shop and was very happy there but that he was ready to leave this position as he had previous ones, glad to do any task, however small, for the love of God.

That for him the time of prayer was no different from any other time, that he retired to pray when Father Prior told him to do so, but that he neither desired nor asked for this since his most absorbing work did not divert him from God.

That as he knew he must love God in all things

41

and as he endeavored to do so, he had no need of a director, but a great need of a confessor to absolve him of his faults. That he was very aware of his faults and was not dismayed by them, that he confessed them to God and did not ask Him to excuse them; but that after doing so he returned in peace to his usual practice of love and adoration.

That he had not consulted anyone about his difficulties but knowing solely by the light of faith that God was present, he directed all his actions to Him, come what would, and that he was willing to lose all for the love of God, as it was well worth it.

That our thoughts spoil everything, that the trouble begins with them; but that we must be careful to reject them as soon as we perceive they are not necessary to what we are doing at the time nor to our salvation, and resume again our conversation with God wherein we attain our greatest well being.

That in the beginning he had often spent the entire time allotted to prayer in resisting his thoughts and then relapsing into them. That he had never been able to pray by rule as others do; that nevertheless at first he had prayed aloud for some time but that afterward he could not recall what had happened.

That he had asked to remain a novice always, not believing anyone would want to profess him, and unable to believe that his two years of novitiate had passed.

That he was not bold enough to ask God for mortifications, that he did not even desire them, but that he was well aware that he deserved them and that when God sent them to him, He would give him the grace to endure them.

That all the mortifications and other exercises are useful only insofar as they bring us to union with God through love; that after having given much thought to the matter, he had concluded the shortest path to God was by a continual exercise of love, while doing all things for the love of God.

That one must carefully differentiate between the actions of the understanding and those of the will; that the former were of little value, and the latter, all; that our only concern was to love and be happy in God.

That all possible mortifications would not erase a single sin if divorced from the love of God. That we should await, without anxiety, the remission of our sins through the blood of Jesus Christ, while trying to love Him with all our heart; that God seemed to choose the greatest sinners, rather than those who had lived in innocence, to bestow His greatest graces on, for by this action was clearly revealed His ineffable goodness.

That he gave no thought to death, nor to his sins, nor to paradise, nor to hell but only to doing little things for the love of God since he was incapable of doing great things; that whatever happened to him after that would not bother him since it was God's will.

That the greatest pains and joys of the world could not be compared with those he had often experienced in the spiritual life; and so he was concerned about nothing and feared nothing, asking of God only one thing, that he not offend Him.

He told me that he had no scruples for "when I know I have failed, I acknowledge it and say, 'that is what I usually do when I am left to myself;' if I have not failed, I give thanks to God, and acknowledge it is His doing."

THIRD CONVERSATION

November 22, 1666

He told me that the foundation of his spiritual
life had been a high idea and esteem of God
through faith, and once he had understood this, he
immediately rejected entirely every other consideration that he might perform all his activities for
the love of God. That when he had not thought of
Him for quite a while he did not let it bother him,
but after having acknowledged his wretchedness to
God, he returned to Him with even more confidence
for having suffered such misery in forgetting Him so.

That the trust we put in God honors Him greatly and draws down on us great graces.

That it was impossible not only that God would deceive but also that He would permit a soul, totally abandoned to Him and resolved to endure all for Him, to suffer for any appreciable length of time.

That he had attained a state wherein he thought only of God and when he felt one or another temptation arising, he felt it coming on and in view of his experience in receiving prompt help from God, he sometimes allowed it to continue until, at the propitious moment, he called on God and the temptation immediately disappeared.

That in view of this, when he had outside business to attend to, he did not think of it ahead of time, but when it was time to take action in the matter, God showed him, as in a mirror, what he should do. That for some time he had been pursuing this course of not expecting any difficulties; that before experiencing God's prompt aid in his affairs he had worried about them ahead of time.

That he gave no thought to those things he had finished with and almost none to those in which he was engaged; that after he had dined, he did not know what he had eaten; but that in acting in his own simple way, he was doing all for the love of God, thanking Him for directing his activities, and doing numerous other acts of love; but all were done very simply in such a way as to keep him in the loving presence of God.

That when some outside matter diverted his mind a bit from thinking of God, he received a reminder from God that invested his soul, giving it so strong a sense of God and so inflaming and transporting it that he cried out, singing and dancing violently like a madman.

That he was more united to God in his ordinary activities than when he devoted himself to religious activities which left him with a profound spiritual dryness.

That he expected shortly some great anguish in body and in spirit and even worse to lose the sense of God which he had experienced so long; but that the goodness of God assured him that He would not forsake him completely and He would give him the strength to withstand any evil that He might allow to happen to him; and therefore he need fear nothing and had no need to discuss his spiritual state with anyone. That when he had tried to do so, he always came away more perplexed, and that since he was willing to give up his life and be lost for the love of God, he felt no apprehension. That complete abandonment to God was the sure way, and one always had light to illumine the way.

That in the beginning of the spiritual life it was necessary to act faithfully and to renounce one's own will; but after that one experiences indescribable happiness. That in difficulties we had only to turn to Jesus Christ and ask for His grace, whereupon everything became easy.

That many become bogged down in penances and particular practices while neglecting love which is the real end; that this can be readily seen in their works; and was the reason we see so little solid virtue.

That neither skill nor knowledge was needed to go to God but only a heart determined to devote itself to Him, for Him, and to love Him only.

FOURTH CONVERSATION
November 25, 1667

Brother Lawrence spoke to me openly and with great fervor of his way of going to God, some of which I have already commented upon.

He told me that it consists of renouncing once and for all everything that we know does not lead to God, so that we might accustom ourselves to a continual conversation with Him, a conversation free of mystery and of the utmost simplicity. That we needed only to know God intimately present in us, to address ourselves to Him at every moment, to ask

His aid, to discern His will in doubtful things, and to do well those things we see clearly He is demanding of us, offering them to Him before doing them and giving Him thanks for having done them for Him after we have done them.

That in this continual conversation we are likewise unceasingly engaged in praising, adoring and loving God for His goodness and perfection.

That relying on the infinite merits of our Lord, we should, with complete confidence, ask for His grace regardless of our sins; that God never failed to grant us His grace at each action; that he perceived this clearly and never failed to do so unless he was distracted from the presence of God, or unless he had forgotten to ask Him for His aid.

That in time of doubt God never failed to enlighten us when we had no other purpose but to please Him and to act for His love.

That our sanctification depended not upon changing our works but in doing for God what we ordinarily do for ourselves. That it was a pity to see how many people always mistake the means for the end, attaching great importance to certain works that they do very imperfectly for reasons of human respect.

That he found the best way of reaching God was by doing ordinary tasks, which he was obliged to perform under obedience, entirely for the love of God and not for the human attitude toward them.

That it was a great delusion to think that time set aside for prayer should be different from other times, that we were equally obliged to be united to

God by work in the time assigned to work as by prayer during prayer time.

That his prayer was simply an awareness of the presence of God, at which time his soul was oblivious to everything else but love; but that afterwards he found no difference, staying close to God by praising Him and blessing Him with all his being so that he passed his life in continual joy, yet hoping God would send him some suffering when he grew strong enough to endure it.

That once and for all we must trust God and abandon ourselves to Him alone, for He would not deceive us.

That we should not weary of doing little things for the love of God who looks not at the grandeur of these actions but rather at the love with which they are performed; that we should not be surprised at failing often in the beginning but that in the end we will acquire a habit which will allow us to perform our acts effortlessly and with great pleasure.

That only faith, hope and charity are needed to become united to the will of God, that all else is unimportant to be used only as a bridge to be passed over quickly in order to lose ourselves by confidence and love in our final destination.

That all things are possible to him who believes, more so to him who hopes [still more to him who loves], and most of all to him who perseveres in the practice of these three virtues.

That the end we ought to propose to ourselves in this life is to become the most perfect adorers of God we possibly can, as we hope to be His perfect adorers through all eternity.

That when we enter upon the spiritual life we should consider in depth who we are, and then we will find we are deserving of all contempt, unworthy of the name Christian, subject to all kinds of miseries and to countless accidents which upset us and cause our health, our temperament, and our disposition, both interior and exterior, to fluctuate—in fact, persons whom God must humble with an infinite variety of sufferings and travail, within as well as without. In view of this is it surprising that we experience pain, temptations, opposition and contradictions from other men? Should we not, on the contrary, submit to these sufferings and bear them as long as God wishes us to as things which are to our advantage?

That the greater perfection a soul aspires to, the more dependent it is upon grace.

LETTERS
FROM BROTHER LAWRENCE
OF THE RESURRECTION TO
SEVERAL RELIGIOUS AND
DEVOUT PERSONS

FIRST LETTER

To Reverend Mother N——

Reverend Mother:

I am taking this opportunity to acquaint you with the reflections of one of our religious on the wonderful effects and the continual assistance he is receiving from the presence of God: let the both of us profit from them.

You should know that his principal concern during his more than forty years in religion has to be with God always, to do nothing, to say nothing and to think nothing that would displease Him; solely for love of Him and because He deserves infinitely more.

He is now so accustomed to this divine presence that he receives continual aid from it in all circumstances; for almost thirty years his soul has been filled with interior joys so continual and sometimes so great that to contain them and prevent their outward manifestation, he has resorted to behavior that seems more foolishness than piety.

If sometimes he strays a bit from that divine presence, God makes Himself felt in his soul to recall it to Him, often when he is engaged in his regular duties; he responds with strict fidelity to these interior entreaties either by lifting up his heart to God, or by a sweet and loving gaze, or by such words as love fashions on these occasions, for example, "My God, here I am, all Yours; Lord make me according to Your heart." And then it seems to him that this God of love, satisfied with these few words, returns and rests again in the very depths of his soul. These experiences make him so certain that God is always in the depths of his soul that there is no longer any doubt in his mind about it under any circumstances.

You may judge from this, Reverend Mother, what contentment and what satisfaction he enjoys; continually having within himself so great a treasure, and no longer suffering the pain and anxiety of looking for and finding it. It is completely revealed and available to him and he may take of it what he pleases.

He complains often of our blindness, constantly crying out that we are to be pitied for our willingness to be satisfied with so little. "God," he says, "has infinite treasures to give us and still we are satisfied with a brief passing moment of piety; that we are blind and by our blindness we restrain the hand of God and so stop the flow of the abundance of His graces. But when He finds a soul imbued with a living faith, He pours into it His graces in abundance. It is like a torrent forcibly diverted from its usual course which having found a passage pours through irresistibly in an overwhelming flood."

Yes, often we restrain this torrent by ignoring it. Let us hold it back no longer, my dear Mother, let us return into ourselves, let us break this dike that dams it, let us make way for grace, let us make up for lost time for perhaps we have little time left to live. Death is close behind us; we die only once so let us be prepared.

Again I say let us return into ourselves; time presses down on us and each man is responsible for himself. I believe you have taken the proper measures and so will not be taken by surprise. I admire you for it, for that is our responsibility.

Nevertheless, we must persevere since in the spiritual life not to advance is to retreat, but those who have been breathed on by the Holy Spirit move forward even while sleeping; if the vessel of our soul is still battered by winds or by storm, let us call on our Lord who rests therein. He will soon calm the sea.

I have taken the liberty, my very dear Mother, of sharing some of these reflections with you so that you may compare them with your own; they will serve to rekindle and inflame yours if, by some misfortune (which God forbid as that would be a great

57

ill), they should have, even if by ever so little, cooled down. Let you and I, then, recall our first fervors, let us profit from the examples and sentiments of this religious little known to the world but known to God and well beloved by Him. I would request that same love for you and earnestly request it for me who am in our Lord,

Yours, etc.

From Paris
June 1, 1682

SECOND LETTER

To Reverend Mother N——

Reverend and most honored Mother:

I received today two books and a letter from Sister N—— who is preparing to make her profession and for this reason asks the prayers of your holy community and yours in particular. She seems to me to have great confidence in them so do not disappoint her. Ask God that she may make her sacrifice solely for His love and with a firm resolution to give herself entirely to Him. I will send you one of these books which treat of the presence of God which in my opinion encompasses the whole spiritual life; and it seems to me that whoever practices it correctly will soon attain the spiritual life.

I know that to achieve this the heart must be emptied of all other things, for God wishes to possess it alone; and as He cannot possess it alone without emptying it of everything that is not Himself, so neither can He act there and do what He wishes there unless it is empty of all else.

There is no mode of life in the world more pleasing and more full of delight than continual conversation with God; only those who practice and experience it can understand it. I do not, however, advise you to pursue it for this purpose. We should not be seeking consolation from this practice, but let us do it motivated by love and because God wishes it.

If I were a preacher, I would preach nothing else but the practice of the presence of God; if I were a director I would recommend it to everyone, so necessary and so easy do I believe it to be.

Ah! If only we knew how we need God's grace and assistance, we would never lose sight of Him not even for an instant. Believe me, from this very moment, make a holy and firm resolution never to be wilfully separated from Him, and to live the rest of your days in His sacred presence deprived, for His love if He deems it proper, of any heavenly or earthly consolation. Get going on this work; if you do as He wishes, be assured you will soon see the results; I will aid you with my prayers, inadequate though they are. I recommend myself earnestly to yours and those of your community, being theirs and more particularly,

Yours, etc.

THIRD LETTER

To the same

Reverend and most honored Mother:

I received from Miss de N—— the rosaries which you gave her for me. I am surprised that you have not told me what you think of the book I sent you; you should have received it by now. Practice its teachings in your old age; it is better late than never.

I cannot understand how religious people can live contented lives without the practice of the presence of God. For myself I withdraw as much as I can to the deepest recesses of my soul with Him, and while

I am thus with Him I fear nothing; but the least turning away from Him is hell for me. This exercise does not weary the body; as a matter of fact it is appropriate from time to time, and even often, to deprive it of many little harmless and allowable pleasures; for God does not allow a soul entirely devoted to Him to have any other pleasure than with Him; this is entirely reasonable.

I am not saying that to do this it is necessary to curb oneself unreasonably; no, we must serve God in a holy freedom; we must do our work faithfully, without distress or anxiety, recalling our mind to God calmly and tranquilly whenever we find it distracted from Him.

It is necessary, however, to put our complete trust in God, putting aside all other cares, even certain devotions which, though very good in themselves, are often engaged in for the wrong reasons, since these devotions are only the means to attain the end. Thus, since by this exercise of the presence of God we are with Him who is our end, it is useless for us to resort to the means; but we can continue our communion of love with Him, living in His holy presence, at one time by an act of adoration, of praise, of desire, at another time by an act of resignation, of thanksgiving, and in any other way our spirit can conceive.

Do not be discouraged by the resistance you will encounter from your human nature; you must go against your human inclinations. Often, in the beginning, you will think that you are wasting time, but you must go on, be determined and persevere in it until death, despite all the difficulties.

I recommend myself to the prayers of your holy community, and to yours in particular, I am, in our Lord,

Yours,

From Paris
November 3, 1685

FOURTH LETTER

To Mrs. N——

Madame:

I deeply sympathize with you. If you can leave the conduct of your affairs to Mr. and Mrs. N—— and devote yourself entirely to praying to God you will have accomplished a great feat. He does not ask much of us, merely a thought of Him from time to time, a little act of adoration, sometimes to ask for His grace, sometimes to offer Him your sufferings, at other times to thank Him for the graces, past and present, He has bestowed on you, in the midst of your troubles to take solace in Him as often as you can. Lift up your heart to Him during your meals and in company; the least little remembrance will always be most pleasing to Him. One need not cry out very loudly; He is nearer to us than we think.

It is not necessary to be always in church to be with God, we can make a private chapel of our heart where we can retire from time to time to commune with Him, peacefully, humbly, lovingly; everyone is capable of these intimate conversations with God, some more, others less; He knows what we can do. Let us begin—perhaps He is only waiting for a single generous resolution from us. Have courage, we have little time to live. You are almost 65 and I am approaching 80; let us live and let us die with God, suffering will always be more sweet and more pleasant when we are with Him, and the greatest pleasures would be a cruel affliction without Him. May He be blessed by all. Amen.

Become accustomed then little by little to adore Him in this way: demand of Him His grace; offer Him your heart from time to time during the day in the midst of your work, at every moment if you can; do not burden yourself with rules or particular devotions but act with faith, with love and with humility.

Assure Mr. and Mrs. N—— and Miss N—— of my poor prayers, and that I am their servant and particularly yours in our Lord,

Brother, etc.

FIFTH LETTER

To Reverend Father N——

My Reverend Father:

Although I do not find my manner of life in books, I am not at all disturbed by this; nevertheless to reinforce my confidence I would appreciate knowing your feelings on the state in which I find myself.

Several days ago in a conversation with a religious person she told me that the spiritual life was a life of grace which begins in servile fear, is increased by the hope of eternal life and is consummated in pure love; that each of these states has different stages by which one finally achieves that blissful consummation.

I have not followed all these methods. On the contrary, I know not why, they discouraged me from the first which was the reason why, on my entrance into religion, I resolved to give myself entirely to God in reparation for my sins, and to renounce everything for His love.

During my early years I meditated in my prayers on death, judgment, hell, paradise and my sins. I continued in this manner for several years, assiduously devoting myself the rest of the day, even during my work, to the presence of God whom I felt was always near me, often in the deepest recesses of my heart, a practice which so heightened my concept of God that only faith was capable of satisfying me about this concept.

Gradually I found myself doing the same thing during the time formally set aside for prayer which caused me great delight and great consolation. I must tell you though that during the first ten years I endured great suffering; the apprehension of not being with God as I wished, my sins constantly on my mind and the great graces which God constantly showered on me, were the cause and source of all my difficulties. During this period I often fell but raised myself up at once. It seemed to me that man, reason and even God Himself were against me and that only faith was for me. I was sometimes troubled by the thought that it was presumptuous of me to think that I had achieved quickly what others achieved only with difficulty; at other times by the thought that I was deliberately damning myself, that there was no salvation for me.

Just as I thought I must live out my life beset by these difficulties and anxieties (which in no way lessened my confidence in God and which only increased my faith) I suddenly found myself changed and my soul, which up till then was always disturbed, experienced a profound interior peace as if it had found its center and a place of peace.

Since that time I have walked before God, in simplicity and faith, with humility and love, and I have labored diligently to do, say and think only what would please Him. I trust that when I have done all that I can He will do with me as He wishes.

As to what I am now experiencing, I cannot express it in words; I have no difficulty with or doubt about my state as I have no other will but God's, which I try to fulfill in everything I do, and to which I am so resigned that I would not lift a straw from the ground except in accordance with His order, or from any other motive than sheer love of Him.

I have given up all my non-obligatory devotions and prayers and concentrate on being always in His holy presence; I keep myself in His presence by simple attentiveness and a loving gaze upon God which I can call the actual presence of God or to put it more clearly, an habitual, silent and secret conversation of the soul with God; which sometimes causes me interior, and often exterior, happiness and joy so great that in order to moderate them and prevent their outward manifestation, I am obliged to resort to behavior that seems more foolishness than piety.

In short, Reverend Father, I have no doubt at all that my soul has been with God for more than thirty years. I pass over many things not to bore you, yet I think it is proper that I indicate to you how I consider myself to be before God whom I look upon as my King.

I regard myself as the most wretched of all men, stinking and covered with sores, and as one who has committed all sorts of crimes against his King. Overcome by remorse, I confess all my wickedness to Him, ask His pardon and abandon myself entirely to Him to do with as He will. But this King, filled with goodness and mercy, far from chastising me, lovingly embraces me, makes me eat at His table, serves me with His own hands, gives me the keys of His treasures and treats me as His favorite. He talks with me and is delighted with me in a thousand and one ways; He forgives me and relieves me of my principal bad habits without talking about them; I beg Him to make me according to His heart and always the more weak and despicable I see myself to be, the more beloved I am of God. That is how I look upon myself from time to time in His holy presence.

My most usual method is this simple attentiveness and this loving gaze upon God to whom I often feel myself united with greater happiness and satisfaction than that of an infant nursing at his mother's breast; also for the inexpressible sweetness which I taste and experience there, if I dared use this term, I would willingly call this state "the breasts of God." If sometimes by necessity or weakness I am distracted from this thought, I am soon recalled to it by interior emotions so delightful and so entrancing that I am ashamed to speak of them. I would beg you, Reverend Father, to reflect on my gross imperfections, of which you are fully aware, rather than on the great graces with which God favors my soul, wholly unworthy and ungrateful as I am.

As for time formally set aside for prayer, it is only a continuation of this same exercise. Sometimes I think of myself as a block of stone before a sculptor, ready to be sculpted into a statue, presenting myself thus to God and I beg Him to form His perfect image in my soul and make me entirely like Himself.

At other times, as soon as I concentrate, and with no trouble or effort on my part, I feel my whole spirit and my whole soul raised up and it remains so as if suspended and firmly fixed in God as its center and place of rest.

I know that some people consider this state as one of idleness, delusion and self-love; I confess it is holy idleness and a happy self-love if the soul in this state were capable of these; but in reality while it is in this state the soul cannot be influenced by the actions one formerly performed; they helped it then but are now more of a hindrance than a help.

In the meantime, I cannot allow this state to be called delusion since the soul which is thus joined to God has no other desire than to be with Him; if this is delusion on my part it is for Him to correct it; let Him do with me as He wishes, I desire only Him and to be wholly His. However, I would appreciate it if you would send me your opinion to which I always defer for I hold your Reverence in the highest esteem, and am in our Lord, my Reverend Father,

Yours, etc.

SIXTH LETTER

To Reverend Mother N——

Reverend and most honored Mother:

Although my prayers are of little value, you will not be without them; I promised you that, I will keep my word. How happy we would be if we could find the treasure of which the Gospel speaks; all else would be as nothing. As it is boundless, the more you search for it the greater are the riches you will find; let us search unceasingly and let us not stop until we have found it.

(He then speaks of several private matters, after which he goes on to say:)

And finally, Reverend Mother, I do not know what I shall become. It seems peace of soul and tranquillity of spirit come to me even in sleep. If I were capable of suffering, there would be none for me to have, and if I were allowed I would gladly submit to the sufferings of purgatory which I would endure in reparation for my sins; I know only that God protects me, I am in a state of tranquillity so sublime that I fear nothing. What could I fear when I am with Him? I hold fast to Him as much as I can; may He be blessed by all, Amen.

Yours, etc.

SEVENTH LETTER
To Mrs. N—

Madame:

We have a God of infinite goodness who knows what we need. I have always thought He would allow you to suffer great afflictions; He will come in His own good time and when you least expect it; hope in Him more than ever, thank Him with me for the graces He has granted you, particularly for the fortitude and patience He is giving you in your afflictions. It is a sure sign of His care for you; take comfort then in Him and thank Him for everything.

I admire also the courage and fortitude of Mr. de N——. God has given him a good disposition and a good will, but he is still a little worldly and very immature; I hope the trial God has sent him will act as a wholesome medicine for him and will make him himself once again. It is an occasion to convince him to put all his trust in Him who is with him everywhere and that he should think of Him as often as he can, especially in the greatest dangers.

A little lifting up of the heart suffices; a little remembrance of God, an interior act of adoration, even though made on the march and with sword in hand, are prayers which, short though they may be, are nevertheless very pleasing to God, and far from making a soldier lose his courage on the most dangerous occasions, bolster it. Let him then think of God as much as possible so that he will gradually become accustomed to this little but holy exercise; no one will notice it and nothing is easier than to repeat often during the day these little acts of interior adoration. Recommend to him, please, that he think of God as often as he can in the way I have explained here: It is a most fitting and necessary practice for a soldier daily in danger of his life and even of his salvation. I hope God will assist him and his family whom I greet and am their and your

Very humble, etc.

October 11, 1688

EIGHTH LETTER
To Reverend Mother N—

Reverend and most honored Mother:

You tell me nothing new, you are not the only one troubled by wandering thoughts; our mind constantly wanders, but the will is mistress of our faculties and must recall it and bring it to God as its last end.

When the mind is untrained from the beginning it has acquired bad habits of wandering and dissipation which are difficult to overcome and usually draw us, even against our will, to worldly things.

I think one remedy for this is to confess our faults and humble ourselves before God; I do not advise much talking in prayer, long discourses often being the cause of wandering. Present yourself in prayer to God like a dumb and paralytic beggar at a rich man's door; concentrate on keeping your mind in the presence of the Lord; if it sometimes wanders and withdraws itself from Him, do not let it upset you; confusion serves rather to distract the mind than to recollect it; the will must bring it back calmly; if you persevere in this way, God will have pity on you.

One way of easily recalling the mind during prayer and keeping it at rest is not to let it wander during the day. You should keep it strictly in the presence of God; and being accustomed to thinking of Him often, it will be easy to keep your mind under control during your prayers or at least to keep it from wandering.

I have already told you at length in my other letters of the advantages found in this practice of the presence of God. Let us apply ourselves to it seriously and pray for each other. I recommend myself also to the prayers of Sister N—— and Reverend Mother N—— and am, in all things, in our Lord,

Very humble, etc.

NINTH LETTER

To the same

Here is a reply to the letter I received from our good Sister N——; please give it to her. She appears to me to be full of good will but she wants to go faster than grace. One does not become holy all at once. I recommend her to you; we ought to help one another with our advice, and still more by our good examples. I would be obliged if you will let me hear of her from time to time, and if she is very fervent and obedient.

Let us often reflect, my dear Mother, that our only concern in this life is to please God: What can anything else be but folly and vanity? You and I have been in the religious life more than forty years. Have we used them to love and to serve God who in His mercy has called us to that state for that purpose? I am filled with shame and embarrassment when I reflect, on the one hand, on the great graces which God has granted me and which He continues without surcease to grant me and, on the other hand, how poorly I have used them and how little I have profited from them on the way to perfection.

Since in His mercy He still gives us a little time, let us begin in earnest, let us make up for lost time, let us return with complete confidence to that Father of goodness who is always ready to receive us lovingly. Let us renounce, my dear Mother, let us renounce fully for His love everything that is not of Himself; He deserves infinitely more; let us think of Him continually, let us put all our confidence in Him. I have no doubt but that we will soon experience the effects of so doing, and that we will receive His graces in abundance with which we can do all and without which we can do nothing but sin.

We cannot avoid the dangers and perils with which life abounds without the actual and unceasing help of God; let us ask His help continually. How can we ask for His help unless we are with Him? How can we be with Him except by thinking of Him often? How can we think of Him often except by forming a holy habit of doing so? You will tell me that I am always saying the same thing to you. It's true. I do not know of an easier or more appropriate method; and as I practice no other, I recommend it to everybody. We must know before we can love; to know God we must often think of Him; and when we come to love Him we shall also think of Him very often, for our heart is where our treasure is!* Let us ponder this often and deeply.

Your very humble, etc.

March 28, 1689

* Translator's note: A play on Matthew 6:21, "For where your treasure is, there will be your heart also."

TENTH LETTER

To Mrs. N——

Madame:

I have had a great deal of difficulty in bringing myself to write to Mr. de N—— I do so only because you and Mrs. de N—— want me to do so. Take the trouble then to put the address on my letter and send it to him.

I am very pleased with the trust you have in God; I hope He will ever increase it. We cannot put too much trust in so good and faithful a friend who will never betray us in this world or the next.

If Mr. de N—— can take advantage of the loss he has suffered and put his trust completely in God, He will soon give him another friend more powerful and more favorably inclined. He disposes of hearts as He pleases; perhaps Mr. de N—— was inordinately attached in a worldly way to the friend he has lost. We ought to love our friends but without prejudicing the love of God which must come first. Remember, I beg you, what I have recommended to you, which is to think often of God, by day, by night, in all your pursuits and duties; even during your recreations. He is always near you and with you; do not leave Him alone. You would think it rude to leave a friend alone who came to visit you. Why abandon God and leave Him alone? Then do not forget Him! Think of Him often, adore Him continually, live and die with Him; that is the glorious business of a Christian; in a word, it is our calling; if we do not know that calling we must learn it. I will help you with my prayers. I am in our Lord,

Your, etc.

From Paris
October 29, 1689

ELEVENTH LETTER

To Reverend Mother N——

Reverend and most honored Mother:

I am not asking God to deliver you from your sufferings, but I do ask Him earnestly to give you the strength and patience to endure them as long as He wishes you to; comfort yourself with Him who keeps you fastened to the Cross; He will release you from it when He deems it proper. Happy are those who suffer with Him; accustom yourself to suffering thus and ask Him for the strength to suffer all that

He wishes and for as long as He decides is necessary. The world does not understand these truths and it doesn't surprise me since worldly people suffer as people of the world do and not as Christians. They regard sickness as an affliction of nature and not as a gift from God: viewed in this light they find in it only the hardness and rigor of nature. But those who look upon sickness as coming from God, as a consequence of His mercy and as a means He employs for their salvation, ordinarily bear it with great contentment and solace.

I wish you could convince yourself that God is often nearer in times of illness and weakness than when we are in a perfect state of health; look for no other doctor but Him. As I understand it, He wishes to cure you Himself; put all your trust in Him and you will soon see the effects of this trust in your recovery which we often retard by relying more on medicines than on God.

I suppose you will tell me that I am very much at ease, eating and drinking at the table of the Lord; you are right; but do you think the biggest criminal in the world could eat at the table of the Lord and be served by His hands completely at ease unless he was assured of His pardon? I think he would experience such great discomfort that only confidence in the goodness of his Sovereign would alleviate it. Also, I can assure you that whatever pleasures I may derive from drinking and eating at the table of my King, the awareness of my sins constantly before me, as well as the uncertainty of my pardon, causes me great suffering though, to tell the truth, that suffering is pleasing to me.

Be satisfied with the state God has designated for you; however happy you may think me, I envy you. My pains and sufferings would be a paradise to me if I suffered them with God, and the greatest pleasures would be a hell if I enjoyed them without Him; all my solace would be to suffer something for Him.

I will soon be going to see God, that is to say I will be rendering my accounting to Him. For if I can see God for a single moment, the sufferings of purgatory would be sweet to me even if they lasted to the end of the world. What comforts me in this life is that I see God by faith in such a manner that I can sometimes say: "I no longer believe, but I see." I experience what faith teaches us; and in that assurance and practice of the faith I will live and die with Him.

Stay always then with God. He alone and only He can alleviate your ills. I will pray that He keep you in His presence. My greetings to Reverend Mother Prioress and I recommend myself to her prayers, to those of her holy community and to yours and am in our Lord

Yours, etc.

This November 17, 1690

TWELFTH LETTER

To Reverend Mother N——

My Reverend Mother:

Since you earnestly wish me to impart to you the method that I have followed to reach this state of the presence of God which our Lord in His mercy has allowed me to attain, I must tell you that it is only with great reluctance that I am giving way to your importunities and only on condition that you will allow no one to see my letter. If I thought you would allow anyone to see it, all my desire for your advancement on the way to perfection would not persuade me to write it. Here is what I can tell you about it.

Having found different methods of going to God and different practices to attain the spiritual life in several books, I decided that they would serve more to hinder than to facilitate me in what I was seeking —which was nothing other than a means to be wholly God's. This made me decide to give all to gain all; so after having given all to God in satisfaction for my sins, I began to live as if there were no one in the world but Him and me. Sometimes I considered myself before Him as a poor criminal at the feet of his judge; at other times I looked on Him in my heart as my Father and as my God. I adored Him as often as I could, keeping my mind in His holy presence and recalling it as often as it wandered. I had no little difficulty in this exercise, but I kept on despite all difficulties and was not worried or distressed when I was involuntarily distracted. I did this during the day as often as I did it during the formal time specifically set aside for prayer; for at all times, at every hour, at every moment, even in the busiest times of my work, I banished and put away from my mind everything capable of diverting me from the thought of God.

This, Reverend Mother, has been my regular practice ever since I entered religion; though I have done so imperfectly and faintheartedly, I have nevertheless received very great advantages from it. I know well that I have received them through the mercy and goodness of the Lord, since we can do nothing without Him, I even less than others. But keeping ourselves faithfully in His holy presence and keeping Him always before us, not only hinders us from offending Him and doing anything that would displease Him, at least voluntarily, it also gives us a holy freedom which allows us to ask Him for the graces we need. Finally, the effect of repeating these acts is that they become more habitual and the presence of God becomes, as it were, more natural. Thank Him, if you please, with me, for His great goodness to me and the great number of graces which He has granted to so miserable a sinner as I am; for which I can never be thankful enough. May He be praised by all. Amen.

I am in our Lord,

Yours, etc.

This letter is undated.

THIRTEENTH LETTER

To Reverend Mother N——

My good Mother:

If we were accustomed to the regular exercise of the presence of God, all the ills of the body would be lessened; God often permits us to suffer a little to purify our souls and to bring us to Him; I cannot understand how a soul that is with God and desires only Him can be capable of suffering; I have enough experience to believe this cannot be so.

Take courage. Offer your sufferings to Him unceasingly and ask Him for the strength to endure them; above all make it a habit to talk with Him often and to let Him slip out of your mind as little as possible. Adore Him in your sufferings, offer yourself to Him from time to time and during your worst sufferings ask Him humbly and lovingly, as a child would of his good father, for acquiescence to His will and for the help of His grace. I will aid you in this with my poor and worthless prayers.

God has several ways of drawing us to Him; sometimes He hides Himself from us, but faith, which alone never fails us in our need, should be our support and the foundation of our trust which should be completely in God.

I do not know what God wishes to do with me, I am always very happy; everybody suffers and I who deserve the most severe punishments, I feel joys so continual and so great that I am scarcely able to contain them.

I would willingly ask God for a part of your sufferings if I did not know my weakness which is so great that if He left me to myself for one moment, I would be the most wretched of all creatures. Nevertheless, I do not know how He could leave me alone since faith brings me so close to Him. He never deserts us unless we desert Him first; let us be fearful of separating ourselves from Him, let us always be with Him and let us live and die with Him.

Pray for me and I will pray for you.

Yours, etc.

November 28, 1690

FOURTEENTH LETTER

To the same

My good Mother:

It grieves me to see you suffering for so long; what lightens somewhat my sympathy for your suffering is that I am convinced it is proof of God's love for you; looked at in this manner it is easy for you to bear; my opinion is you should stop all human remedies and abandon yourself entirely to divine Providence. Perhaps He is only waiting for this abandonment and complete trust in Him to cure you; since in spite of all your efforts these remedies have not been effective and, on the contrary, your ills have increased, it is not tempting God then to put yourself in His hands and expect all things from Him.

I have already told you in my last letter that He sometimes permits the body to suffer to cure the illness of our souls; be courageous, make a virtue of necessity. Ask God not to be delivered from the sufferings of your body but for the strength to suffer courageously all that He wishes you to for His love and for as long as it pleases Him.

A prayer such as this is in truth a little difficult for our human nature but is very pleasing to God and sweet to those who love Him. Love eases pain and when one loves God, one suffers for Him with joy and with courage. Do, I beg you, comfort yourself with Him who is the one and only remedy for all our ills. He is the Father of the afflicted, always ready to aid us, and He loves us infinitely more than we imagine. Love Him then and do not seek any other solace than Him; I hope you will receive it soon.

Farewell. I will help you with my prayers, poor as they are, and I shall be always in our Lord

Yours, etc.

P.S. This morning, the feast of St. Thomas, I offered Communion for your intention.

FIFTEENTH LETTER

To the same
To my very dear Mother N——

My very dear Mother:

I give thanks to the Lord to see you are somewhat better, as you wished. I have been near death several times and have never been so content as then; and so I did not ask for relief but rather for the strength to suffer courageously, humbly and lovingly. Take courage, my dear Mother! Ah, how sweet it is to suffer with God! However great the suffering may be, endure it with love; it is paradise to suffer and be with Him. Also, if we wish to enjoy the peace of paradise in this life, we must accustom ourselves to an intimate, humble and loving conversation with Him; we must prevent our minds from wandering away from Him on any occasion; we must make our hearts a sanctuary where we adore Him continually; we must ever be on the alert not to do anything, say anything or think anything that might displease Him. When we are thus occupied with God, suffering will be full of sweetness, a balm and a consolation.

I know that to arrive at this state the beginning is very difficult, that we must act entirely in faith; we also know that we can do all with the grace of the Lord and He does not withhold His grace from those who earnestly ask Him for it. Knock on His door and keep on knocking and I assure you that if you are not discouraged, He will open it in His own good time and will give you all at once what He has withheld for years.

Farewell. Pray to Him for me as I pray to Him for you. I hope to see Him soon. I am yours in our Lord.

January 22, 1691

SIXTEENTH LETTER

To the same

My good Mother:

God knows best what we need and everything He does is for our good; if we knew how much He loves us, we would always be ready to receive from Him, with equanimity, the sweet and the bitter, and even the most painful and most difficult trials would be pleasing and agreeable. The worst afflictions ordinarily are unbearable only when viewed in the wrong way; and when we believe that it is the hand of God acting on us, that it is a Father filled with love who subjects us to this humiliation, grief and suffering then all the bitterness of these tribulations is forgotten and we rejoice in them.

Let us devote ourselves entirely to knowing God; the more we know Him the more we want to know Him; knowledge is commonly the measure of love, the deeper and wider our knowledge, the greater will be our love, and if our love of God is great, we will love Him equally in sorrow and in joy.

Let us not be satisfied with loving God because of the graces He has given us or may give us, however great they may be; these favors, great though they are, will never bring us as near to Him as does one simple act of faith; let us seek Him often by faith. He is in the midst of us; we do not need to seek Him elsewhere. Are we not ill-mannered, even culpable, to leave Him alone, while we busy ourselves with a thousand and one trivial matters which displease Him and perhaps even offend Him? Though He tolerates them, it is to be feared that one day they will cost us dearly.

Let us begin to be devoted to Him in earnest, banishing from our hearts and minds all else; He wishes to be there alone, let us ask this grace of Him; if on our part we do the best we can, we will soon see in ourselves the changes that we are hoping for. I cannot thank Him enough for the little relief He has given you. I hope through His mercy the grace of seeing Him in a few days;* let us pray for one another.

I am in our Lord,

Yours, etc.

February 6, 1691

* Translator's note: God granted him his wish and six days later Brother Lawrence returned to Him.

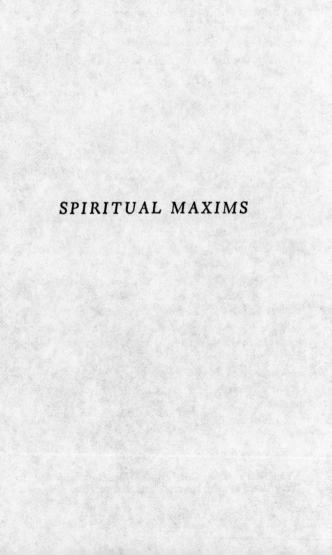

SPIRITUAL MAXIMS

All things are possible to him who believes, more to him who hopes, still more to him who loves and most of all to him who perseveres in the practice of these three virtues; all those who are baptized and believe have taken the first step on the road to perfection and may become perfect if they persevere in the practice of the following maxims:

1. Always see God and His glory in everything we do, say, and undertake; that the end we should seek is to be the most perfect adorers of God in this life, as we hope to be through all eternity; take a firm resolution to overcome, with God's grace, all the difficulties which are met in the spiritual life.

2. When we enter upon the spiritual life, we should consider in depth who we are and we will

99

find ourselves deserving of all contempt, unworthy of the name Christian, subject to all kinds of miseries and countless accidents which upset us and cause our health, our temperament and our disposition, both interior and exterior, to fluctuate—in short, persons whom God must humble with an infinite variety of suffering and travails, within as well as without.

3. We must believe unquestioningly that this is for our own good, that it is pleasing to God to sacrifice ourselves to Him, that it is by His divine Providence that we are abandoned to all kinds of conditions, to suffer all kinds of sufferings, miseries and temptations for the love of God, as long as it pleases Him, since without this submission of the heart and mind to the will of God, devotion and perfection cannot exist.

4. The greater the perfection a soul seeks, the more dependent it is on grace, and the help of God is more necessary for it each moment for without it the soul can do nothing; the world, human nature and the devil together wage a war so fierce and so continual that without this actual help and this humble and necessary dependence, they will carry the soul away in spite of itself; this seems hard on human nature but grace makes it acceptable and a refuge.

PRACTICES NECESSARY
TO ATTAIN THE
SPIRITUAL LIFE

1. The holiest, most common, most necessary practice in the spiritual life is the presence of God, that is to take delight in and become accustomed to His divine company, speaking humbly and talking lovingly with Him at all times, at every moment, without rule or system and especially in times of temptation, suffering, spiritual aridity, disgust and even of unfaithfulness and sin.

2. We must continually work hard so that each of our actions is a way of carrying on little conversations with God, not in any carefully prepared way but as it comes from the purity and simplicity of the heart.

3. We must carry out all of our actions with care and with wisdom, without the impetuosity and precipitancy of a distraught mind; it is necessary to work peacefully, tranquilly and lovingly with God, begging Him to accept our work, and by this continual mindfulness of God we shall crush the head of

the devil and cause his weapons to fall from his hands.

4. During our work and other activities, during our spiritual reading and writing, even more so during our formal devotions and spoken prayers we should stop as often as we can, for a moment, to adore God from the bottom of our hearts, to savor Him, by stealth as it were, as He passes by. Since you know God is with you in all your actions, that He is in the deepest recesses of your soul, why not, from time to time, leave off your external activities and even your spoken prayers to adore Him inwardly, to praise Him, to petition Him, to offer Him your heart and to give Him thanks?

What can be more agreeable to God than to withdraw thus many times a day from the things of man to retire into ourselves and adore Him interiorly; in addition these interior retreats to God gradually free us by destroying that self love which can exist only among our fellow human beings.

And finally, we can give God no greater witness of our fidelity than in renouncing and despising time and again material things to be with our Creator for a single moment.

I do not by this mean that you should always set aside your external activities, that is not possible; but prudence, which is the mother of the virtues, can guide you; nevertheless, I say that it is a common error among spiritual persons not to leave the external world to adore God inwardly and to enjoy peacefully a few moments of His divine presence.

This digression has been lengthy but I thought

the matter deserved this full explanation. Let us return to our practices.

5. All these acts of adoration should be made by faith, knowing that God is truly in our hearts, that we must adore, love and serve Him in spirit and in truth, that He sees everything that happens and will happen to us and to all His creatures, that He is independent of everything and all creatures depend on Him; He is infinitely perfect and by His infinite excellence and sovereign domain deserves our whole beings and everything in heaven and on earth, all of which He can dispose as He pleases in time and in eternity; in justice we owe Him all our thoughts, our words and our actions. Let us make sure we do so.

6. We must carefully ascertain what virtues we most need, which are the most difficult to acquire, the sins we fall into most often, and the most frequent and unavoidable occasions of such falls; in times of temptation we should have recourse to God with complete confidence, remain steadfast in the presence of His Divine Majesty, adore Him humbly, tell Him of our troubles and weaknesses and ask Him lovingly for the help of His grace, and we will find in Him all the virtues we ourselves lack.

HOW WE MUST ADORE GOD IN SPIRIT AND IN TRUTH

There are three points to be considered in this question:

1. To adore God in spirit and in truth means to adore God as we ought to; God is a spirit, therefore He must be worshipped in spirit and in truth; that is to say, by a humble and genuine act of adoration from the very depths of our soul. Only God can see this adoration which if repeated often will eventually become natural for us as if God were one with our soul and our soul one with God: practice will make us understand this.

2. To adore God in truth is to know Him for what He is and to know ourselves for what we are; to adore God in truth is to know truly, certainly and with all our being that God is that which He is, that is infinitely perfect, infinitely adorable, infinitely removed from evil and therefore with all the divine attributes: What man, unreasonable though he may be, would not use all his strength to offer all his reverence and adoration to this mighty God?

3. To adore God in truth is to acknowledge that we are completely the opposite to Him and that He

wishes very much to make us like Him if we wish it; who would be so imprudent to withhold even for a moment the respect, the love, the service and the continual adoration we owe Him?

OF THE UNION
OF THE SOUL
WITH GOD

There are three kinds of union—habitual, virtual and actual.

1. Habitual grace is when one is united to God solely by grace.

2. Virtual union is when one begins an action by which one is united to God and remains united to Him by virtue of this action all the time it continues.

3. Actual union is the most perfect and, since it is entirely spiritual, makes its movement felt because the soul is not passive as in the other unions but is tremendously agitated and its operation is more fiery than that of fire and more brilliant than the sun on a clear day. Nevertheless, one can be misled by this feeling which is not a simple expression of the heart, as when we say: "My God, I love you with all my

heart," or when we use similar other words; but it is, I know not how to say it, something of the soul, sweet, peaceful, spiritual, reverent, humble, loving and very simple, which lifts the soul to God and impels it to love Him, to adore Him, even to embrace Him with an inexplicable tenderness that can be understood only when experienced.

4. All who aspire to the divine union should know that whatever can divert the will to Him is in fact agreeable and pleasing, as the will makes it so.

Everyone must acknowledge that God is incomprehensible and that to unite ourselves to Him the will must be deprived of all sorts of tastes and pleasures, spiritual and corporal, so that being so divested it can love God above all things; for if the will can in any way comprehend God, it can do so only by love. There is a great difference between the tastes and feelings of the will and the workings of that same will since the tastes and feelings of the will are in the soul as in their limits, and its operation, which properly is love, finds its terminus in God as its end.

OF THE PRESENCE OF GOD

1. The presence of God is the applying of our spirit to God, or a realization of the presence of God, which can be brought about either by the imagination or by understanding.

2. I know a person who for forty years has practiced the presence of God intellectually but gives it several other names; sometimes he calls it a simple act or a clear and distinct knowledge of God; at other times an indistinct vision or a loving gaze, a sense of God; still other times he calls it a waiting on God, a silent conversation with God, trust in God, the life and peace of the soul; finally this person told me that all of these expressions for the presence of God, which has come to be natural with him, are only synonyms that express the same thing in this way:

3. By force of habit and by frequently calling his mind to the presence of God, he has developed such a habit that as soon as he is free from his external affairs, and even often while he is deeply immersed in them, the very heart of his soul, with no effort on his part, is raised up above all things and stays suspended and held there in God as in its center and

its place of rest; nearly always, experiencing his soul in this state, and backed up by faith, satisfied him; and it is this that he calls the actual presence of God, which includes all the other kinds of the presence of God and much more as well so that he lives now as if only God and himself were in the world, conversing always with God, asking Him for what he needs and continually rejoicing with Him in a thousand and one ways.

4. Nevertheless, it should be pointed out that this conversation with God is held in the deepest recesses and the very center of the soul; it is there that the soul talks with God heart to heart, and always in a most sublime peace in which the soul rejoices in God; everything that takes place outside is no more to the soul than as a fire of straw which burns itself out as it gives light, and these exterior affairs seldom, or very slightly, disturb its interior peace.

5. But to return to our consideration of the presence of God, I tell you that this sweet and loving gaze of God insensibly kindles a divine fire in the soul which is set ablaze so ardently with the love of God that one is obliged to perform exterior acts to moderate it.

6. We would be very surprised if we knew what the soul sometimes says to God, who seems to be so pleased with these conversations that He allows anything to the soul provided that it wishes to be always with Him and in His heart; and as if He feared that it would return to human things, He takes care to provide it with all its desires so well that it often finds within itself a most delectable and most appe-

tizing banquet though it has done nothing at all to obtain it except by consenting to it.

7. The presence of God is, then, the life and nourishment of the soul which can acquire it by our Lord's grace by these means:

WAYS OF ACQUIRING THE PRESENCE OF GOD

1. The first way is a great purity of life.

2. The second is a great faithfulness to the practice of His presence and an interior gaze on God which should always be quiet, humble and loving without succumbing to any difficulties or disquietude.

3. It is necessary to take particular care to begin, if only for a moment, your exterior actions with this interior gaze and that you do the same while you are doing them and when you have finished them. Since it is necessary to devote much time and effort to acquiring this habit you must not be discouraged when you fail since the habit is formed only with difficulty; but once you have acquired it, you will experience great joy.

Is it not right that the heart which is the seat of

life and which governs the other parts of the body should be the first and the last to love and adore God, should be the beginning and the ending of our activities, spiritual and corporal, and in general through all life's works? And it is the heart which can affect this little interior gaze which, as I have already said, can be brought about when done spontaneously and without study.

4. It would be pertinent for those who undertake this practice to make up interiorly short ejaculations such as: "My God, I am all yours," "God of love, I love You with all my heart," "Lord, make me according to Your heart," and any such words that love may beget on the spur of the moment. But they must be careful that the mind does not wander and return again to worldly things; they should stay close to God alone so that the mind, urged and impelled by the will, is forced to stay with God.

5. This presence of God, though a bit painful in the beginning, if practiced faithfully, works secretly in the soul and produces marvelous effects and draws down to it in abundance the graces of the Lord and leads it insensibly to the simple gaze, that loving sight of God everywhere present, which is the most holy, the most solid, the easiest, the most efficacious manner of prayer.

6. Notice, if you please, that to attain this state you must take for granted the mortification of the senses since it is impossible for a soul still attached to worldly pleasures to be completely joined to this divine presence since to be with God requires complete rejection of worldly things.

THE BENEFITS OF THE
PRESENCE OF GOD

1. The first benefit the soul receives from the presence of God is that faith becomes more alive and more active in every occasion of our life, particularly in our times of need, since it readily obtains grace for us in our temptations and in our unavoidable dealings with our fellow men; for the soul, accustomed by this exercise to rely on faith, by a simple act of recollection sees and feels God present, calls on Him freely and efficaciously, and obtains what it needs. You could say that doing this enables the soul to approach the state of the Blessed; the more it advances, the more alive its faith becomes, and finally it becomes so penetrating that the soul can almost say: "I no longer believe, since I see and I experience."

2. The practice of the presence of God strengthens us in our hope; our hope grows in proportion to our knowledge; to the extent that our faith by this holy practice penetrates the mysteries of the divinity, to that extent does it discover in God a beauty that surpasses infinitely not only that

of the bodies we see on earth but that of the most perfect souls and that of the angels; and so our hope grows and is strengthened, encouraged and sustained by the grandeur of this good which it desires to enjoy and that in some way it savors.

3. It inspires in the will a contempt of worldly things and inflames it with the fire of divine love which, coming from God, is a consuming fire that reduces to ashes whatever is opposed to it; and this soul thus inflamed can live only in the presence of its God, a presence which produces in the heart a holy ardor, a sacred eagerness and a fervent desire to see this God, loved, known, served and adored by all creatures.

4. By the presence of God and by this interior gaze, the soul comes to know God in such a way that it passes almost all its life in making continual acts of love, adoration, contrition, trust, actions of grace, offering, petition and of all the most excellent virtues; and sometimes it even becomes one endless act because the soul is always engaged in staying in this divine presence.

I know you will find few persons attain this state; it is a grace which God grants only to certain chosen souls since this simple gaze is a gift freely bestowed by Him; but I will say for the consolation of those who wish to undertake this holy practice that He usually gives it to souls which are disposed in that direction, and if He does not give it, one can at least, with the help of His ordinary graces, acquire by the practice of the presence of God a way and a state of prayer which very closely approaches this simple gaze.

OTHER IMAGE BOOKS

ABANDONMENT TO DIVINE PROVIDENCE – Jean Pierre de Caussade. Trans. by John Beevers

AGING: THE FULFILLMENT OF LIFE – Henri J. M. Nouwen and Walter J. Gaffney

AMERICAN CATHOLIC EXPERIENCE: A HISTORY FROM COLONIAL TIMES TO THE PRESENT – Jay P. Dolan

AUTOBIOGRAPHY OF ST. THÉRÈSE OF LISIEUX: THE STORY OF A SOUL – New Trans. by John Beevers

BIRTH OF THE MESSIAH – Raymond E. Brown

BREAKTHROUGH: MEISTER ECKHART'S CREATION SPIRITUALITY IN A NEW TRANSLATION – Intro. and Commentary by Matthew Fox

CALLED TO HEAL – Fr. Ralph A. DiOrio

THE CATHOLIC CATECHISM – John A. Hardon, S.J.

CELEBRATING THE SINGLE LIFE – Susan Muto

CENTERING PRAYER – M. Basil Pennington, O.C.S.O.

CHRISTIAN LIFE PATTERNS – Evelyn and James Whitehead

CHRIST IS ALIVE – Michel Quoist

THE CHURCH – Hans Küng

CITY OF GOD – St. Augustine—Ed. by Vernon J. Bourke. Intro. by Étienne Gilson

THE CLOUD OF UNKNOWING (and THE BOOK OF PRIVY COUNSELING) – Newly ed., with an Intro., by William Johnston, S.J.

CLOWNING IN ROME – Henri J. M. Nouwen

COMPASSION – Donald P. McNeill, Douglas A. Morrison, Henri J. M. Nouwen

A CONCISE HISTORY OF THE CATHOLIC CHURCH (Revised Edition) – Thomas Bokenkotter

THE CONFESSIONS OF ST. AUGUSTINE – Trans., with an Intro., by John K. Ryan

CONJECTURES OF A GUILTY BYSTANDER – Thomas Merton

CONTEMPLATIVE PRAYER – Thomas Merton

COVENANT OF LOVE – Richard M. Hogan and John M. LeVoir

CREATIVE MINISTRY – Henri J. M. Nouwen

OTHER IMAGE BOOKS

CROSSWAYS – Fulton J. Sheen

A CRY FOR MERCY – Henri J. M. Nouwen

DAILY WE FOLLOW HIM – M. Basil Pennington, O.C.S.O.

DAILY WE TOUCH HIM – M. Basil Pennington, O.C.S.O.

DARK NIGHT OF THE SOUL – St. John of the Cross. Ed. and trans. by E. Allison Peers

DOORS TO THE SACRED – Joseph Martos

ESSENTIAL CATHOLICISM – Thomas Bokenkotter

ETERNAL LIFE? – Hans Küng

FREE TO BE HUMAN – Eugene Kennedy

GENESEE DIARY – Henri J. M. Nouwen

GOD LOVE YOU – Fulton J. Sheen

THE HEALING POWER OF AFFIRMATION – Fr. Ralph A. DiOrio

HE LEADETH ME – Walter J. Ciszek, S.J., with Daniel Flaherty, S.J.

A HISTORY OF PHILOSOPHY – Frederick Copleston, S.J.
Complete and unabridged in three Image Books

Book One: Volume I – Greece and Rome
             Volume II – Medieval Philosophy (Augustine to Duns Scotus)
             Volume III – Late Medieval and Renaissance Philosophy (Ockham to Suarez)

Book Two: Volume IV – Modern Philosophy (Descartes to Leibniz)
             Volume V – Modern Philosophy (The British Philosophers Hobbes to Hume)
             Volume VI – Modern Philosophy (The French Enlightenment to Kant)

Book Three: Volume VII – Modern Philosophy (Fichte to Nietzsche)
             Volume VIII – Modern Philosophy (Bentham to Russell)
             Volume IX – Modern Philosophy (Maine de Biran to Sarte)

OTHER IMAGE BOOKS

THE IMITATION OF CHRIST – Thomas à Kempis. Ed., with Intro., by Harold C. Gardiner, S.J.

IN HIS FOOTSTEPS – Fr. Ralph A. DiOrio

INTERIOR CASTLE – St. Teresa of Avila – Trans. and ed. by E. Allison Peers

INTRODUCTION TO THE DEVOUT LIFE – St. Francis de Sales. Trans. and ed. by John K. Ryan

INTRODUCTION TO THE NEW TESTAMENT – Raymond F. Collins

I'VE MET JESUS CHRIST – Michel Quoist

THE JOY OF BEING HUMAN – Eugene Kennedy

LIFE AND HOLINESS – Thomas Merton

LIFE IS WORTH LIVING – Fulton J. Sheen

THE LIFE OF ALL LIVING – Fulton J. Sheen

LIFE OF CHRIST – Fulton J. Sheen

LIFE OF TERESA OF JESUS: THE AUTOBIOGRAPHY OF ST. TERESA OF AVILA – Trans. and ed. by E. Allison Peers

THE LITTLE WORLD OF DON CAMILLO – Giovanni Guareschi

MARRYING WELL – Evelyn and James Whitehead

MEDITATION IN MOTION – Susan Muto

MIRACLE OF LOURDES – Updated and Expanded Edition by the Medical Bureau of Lourdes – Ruth Cranston

A MIRACLE TO PROCLAIM – Fr. Ralph A. DiOrio

MODELS OF THE CHURCH – Avery Dulles

MODELS OF REVELATION – Avery Dulles, S.J.

THE MONASTIC JOURNEY – Thomas Merton

NEW GENESIS – Robert Muller

THE NEW TESTAMENT OF THE NEW JERUSALEM BIBLE

NOTHING SHORT OF A MIRACLE: THE HEALING POWER OF THE SAINTS – Patricia Treece

ONE MINUTE WISDOM – Anthony de Mello

ORTHODOXY – G. K. Chesterton

OUR LADY OF FATIMA – William Thomas Walsh

THE PAIN OF BEING HUMAN – Eugene Kennedy

PEACE OF SOUL – Fulton J. Sheen

THE PERFECT JOY OF ST. FRANCIS – Felix Timmermans

OTHER IMAGE BOOKS

PERSONALITY AND SPIRITUAL FREEDOM – Robert and Carol Ann Faucett

POCKET BOOK OF PRAYERS – M. Basil Pennington, O.C.S.O.

POCKET CATHOLIC DICTIONARY – John A. Hardon, S.J.

POCKET DICTIONARY OF SAINTS – John J. Delaney

POPE JOHN XXIII – Peter Hebblethwaite

THE PRACTICE OF THE PRESENCE OF GOD – Trans. with an Intro. by John J. Delaney

PRAYERTIMES: MORNING-MIDDAY-EVENING – M. Basil Pennington, O.C.S.O.

THE PSALMS OF THE JERUSALEM BIBLE – Alexander Jones, General Editor

QUESTION AND ANSWER CATHOLIC CATECHISM – John A. Hardon, S.J.

QUOTABLE CHESTERTON: A TOPICAL COMPILATION OF THE WIT, WISDOM AND SATIRE OF G. K. CHESTERTON

REACHING OUT – Henri J. M. Nouwen

RECONCILIATION: CELEBRATING GOD'S HEALING FORGIVENESS – Rev. Chris Aridas

REJOICE! – Fulton J. Sheen

REVELATIONS OF DIVINE LOVE – Juliana of Norwich. Trans. with Intro. by M. L. del Mastro

THE RULE OF ST. AUGUSTINE – Trans. by Raymond Canning, OSA; Intro. and Commentary by Tarcisius J. Van Bavel, OSA

THE RULE OF ST. BENEDICT – Trans. and ed., with an Intro., by Anthony C. Meisel and M. L. del Mastro

SADHANA: A WAY TO GOD – Anthony de Mello, S.J.

ST. FRANCIS OF ASSISI – G. K. Chesterton

ST. FRANCIS OF ASSISI – Johannes Jorgensen

ST. THOMAS AQUINAS – G. K. Chesterton

SAINTS FOR ALL SEASONS – Ed. by John J. Delaney

SEASONS OF STRENGTH – Evelyn and James Whitehead

A SENSE OF LIFE, A SENSE OF SIN – Eugene Kennedy

SENSING YOUR HIDDEN PRESENCE – Ignacio Larranaga, O.F.M.

OTHER IMAGE BOOKS

THE SHROUD OF TURIN (Revised Edition) – Ian Wilson

SIGNS AND WONDERS: FIRSTHAND EXPERIENCES OF HEALING – Fr. Ralph DiOrio

SONG OF THE BIRD – Anthony de Mello, S.J.

THE SPIRITUAL EXERCISES OF ST. IGNATIUS – Trans. by Anthony Mottola, Ph.D. Intro. by Robert W. Gleason, S.J.

THE STAIRWAY OF PERFECTION – Trans. and ed. by M. L. del Mastro

THE STORY OF THE TRAPP FAMILY SINGERS – Maria Augusta Trapp

SUCH A VISION OF THE STREET – Eileen Egan

THOMAS MERTON ON MYSTICISM – Raymond Bailey

THOMAS MERTON ON PRAYER – John J. Higgins, S.J.

A THOMAS MERTON READER – Revised Edition – Ed. by Thomas P. McDonnell

THROUGH THE YEAR WITH FRANCIS OF ASSISI – Murray Bodo, O.F.M.

THROUGH THE YEAR WITH THOMAS MERTON – Edited by Thomas P. McDonnell

THROUGH THE YEAR WITH THE SAINTS – M. Basil Pennington, O.C.S.O.

A TIME FOR BEING HUMAN – Eugene Kennedy

A TIME FOR LOVE – Eugene Kennedy

TREASURE IN CLAY – The Autobiography of Fulton J. Sheen

THE TROUBLE WITH BEING HUMAN – Eugene Kennedy

THE WAY OF PERFECTION – St. Teresa of Avila. Trans. and ed. by E. Allison Peers

THE WAY OF A PILGRIM (AND THE PILGRIM CONTINUES HIS WAY) – Trans. by Helen Bacovcin

THE WAY OF ST. FRANCIS – Murray Bodo, O.F.M.

WITH GOD IN RUSSIA – Walter J. Ciszek, S.J., with Daniel L. Flaherty, S.J.

A WOMAN CLOTHED WITH THE SUN – Ed. by John J. Delaney

THE WORLD'S FIRST LOVE – Fulton J. Sheen

THE WOUNDED HEALER – Henri J. M. Nouwen

OTHER IMAGE BOOKS

YOUR CATHOLIC WEDDING: A Complete Plan Book – Rev. Chris Aridas